Dear Parent:
Your child's love of reading starts here!

Every child learns to read in a different way and at his or her own speed. Some go back and forth between reading levels and read favourite books again and again. Others read through each level in order. You can help your young reader improve and become more confident by encouraging his or her own interests and abilities. From books your child reads with you to the first books he or she reads alone, there are I Can Read Books for every stage of reading:

SHARED READING
Basic language, word repetition, and whimsical illustrations, ideal for sharing with your emergent reader

BEGINNING READING
Short sentences, familiar words, and simple concepts for children eager to read on their own

READING WITH HELP
Engaging stories, longer sentences, and language play for developing readers

READING ALONE
Complex plots, challenging vocabulary, and high-interest topics for the independent reader

ADVANCED READING
Short paragraphs, chapters, and excitir͏g ͏emes for the perfect bridge to chapt͏er books

I Can Read Books ha͏e ͏n͏ ͏ ͏ ͏y of reading since 1957. Featuring aw͏ ͏ ͏and ͏ustrators and a fabulous cast of beloved c͏ ͏ ͏ad Books set the standard for beginning rea͏d

A lifetime of discovery begins with the magical words **"I Can Read!"**

Visit www.icanread.ca for information
on enriching your child's reading experience.

I Can Read Book® is a trademark of HarperCollins Publishers

The Best First Game
Text copyright © 2019 by HarperCollins Publishers Ltd.
Illustrations © 2019 by Nick Craine.
All rights reserved. Published by Collins, an imprint of HarperCollins Publishers Ltd

HarperCollins books may be purchased for educational, business, or sales promotional use through our Special Markets Department.

HarperCollins Publishers Ltd
Bay Adelaide Centre, East Tower
22 Adelaide Street West, 41st Floor
Toronto, Ontario, Canada
M5H 4E3

www.harpercollins.ca

Library and Archives Canada Cataloguing in Publication information is available upon request.

www.icanread.ca

ISBN 978-1-4434-5730-9

WZL 1 2 3 4 5 6 7 8 9 10

I Can Read!

READING
2
WITH HELP

THE BEST

FIRST GAME

by Meg Braithwaite

Illustrations by Nick Craine

Collins

Auston stepped up to the plate.

The pitcher threw the ball.

Auston swung his bat.

Auston hit a home run!

Auston went up to bat again.

He hit another home run.

Auston's team won the game.

"Can you play tomorrow?"
asked Auston's baseball coach.
"Sorry, coach," said Auston.
"I have a hockey game."

Auston liked baseball.

But he was really good at

hockey too.

"Dad, I love hockey," said Auston.

"Maybe even more than baseball."

Auston smiled.

"Can I play hockey all the time?"

Auston stopped playing baseball.

Now he could play hockey every day.

Auston scored goal after goal.

He got good enough

to join the NHL.

The Toronto Maple Leafs
had first pick in the NHL draft.
They chose Auston.

It was time for Auston's
very first NHL game.
The Toronto Maple Leafs were facing
the Ottawa Senators.

The game started.

Auston skated across the ice.

Auston got his stick on the puck.

He shot it past the goalie

with a flick of his wrist.

A goal!

Auston had scored a goal!

His teammates said, "Great job!"

His parents whistled from the crowd.

But there was no time to celebrate.

The game was starting up again.

The Senators took the puck.

They tied the game quickly.

Then they scored again!

Auston skated as fast as he could
to get to the puck.
First, he pushed it through
Number 68's legs.
Then he got it for himself.

Finally, he skated toward the net

and shot the puck.

His second goal!

The second period started.

The teams were tied.

Soon, Auston got the puck again.

He was right in front of the net.

He took a shot and scored.

Three goals. Auston got a hat trick!

The crowd roared.

They threw their hats onto the ice.

Auston's mom watched from her seat.

She was so happy,

she burst into tears.

The two teams kept fighting

for the puck.

The second period was almost over.

The Senators tied the score again.

Then, something incredible happened.

Auston got the puck right before

the buzzer made

its loud buzzing sound.

Auston skated closer to the net.

He snapped the puck past the goalie!

FOUR

The puck went right in.

His fourth goal!

Auston had done something amazing.

Other players had scored hat tricks

in their very first games.

But no one had ever scored

four goals like Auston had.

The score was tied after
the third period.

Then the game went into overtime.

And the Senators scored.

The Senators won the game

by one goal.

Auston was disappointed

that the Leafs hadn't won.

But he had broken a hockey record.

He played the best first game ever.